Thirty Day Affirmations AND Manifestations for Women 50 & Over

Thirty Day Affirmations And Manifestations for Women 50 & Over. Copyright 2022 by Deborah Ware. All rights reserved. No part of this publication may be reproduced, distributed, or transmitted in any form or by any means, including photocopying, recording, or other electronic or mechanical methods, without the prior written permission of the publisher, except in the case of brief quotations embodied in critical reviews and certain other noncommercial uses permitted by copyright law.

For permission requests, write to the publisher, addressed "Attention: Permissions Coordinator," 205 N. Michigan Avenue, Suite #810, Chicago, IL 60601. 13th & Joan books may be purchased for educational, business or sales promotional use. For information, please email the Sales Department at sales@13thandjoan.com.

Printed in the U. S. A.
First Printing, July 2022.
Library of Congress Cataloging-in-Publication Data has been applied for.

ISBN: 978-1-953156-64-8

I DEDICATE MY BOOK OF 30 DAY AFFIRMATIONS TO A POWERFUL African American Woman that uses her heart and passion for writing helping to inspire others to tell their stories. Ardre Orie, CEO, and Founder of 13th & Joan Publishing House gave me the courage and inspiration to recognize that I had a story to tell. By sharing my story, I could help others overcome obstacles in their lives that held them back from letting their dreams come full circle.

Ardre Orie inspired me to not be afraid to find my niche and use it to inspire those that wanted to be inspired and set themselves free from needing validation to follow their dreams. I have gained my self-worth, my self-esteem has soared, and I am a stronger, more confident woman with a powerful purpose. I recognized that I only need validation from myself, dream freely, and feel empowered to empower other women around me to realize that they matter.

Today I stand tall without being afraid to demonstrate the love I have for myself. Thank you, Ardre Orie, for being such a beautiful role model of a strong and powerful African American Queen that continues to encourage others to set their stories free.

Deborah Ware

Contents

INTRODUCTION 1
A GUIDE TO USING MY JOURNAL 3
DAILY QUICK STEPS TO GETTING STARTED 4
10 SUGGESTED PLACES TO POST YOUR AFFIRMATION FOR THE DAY AS A REMINDER OF SELF LOVE. 5

DAY 1 6	DAY 14 32
DAY 2 8	DAY 15 34
DAY 3 10	DAY 16 36
DAY 4 12	DAY 17 38
DAY 5 14	DAY 18 40
DAY 6 16	DAY 19 42
DAY 7 18	DAY 20 44
DAY 8 20	DAY 21 46
DAY 9 22	DAY 22 48
DAY 10 24	DAY 23 50
DAY 11 26	DAY 24 52
DAY 12 28	DAY 25 54
DAY 13 30	DAY 26 56

| DAY 27 | 58 | DAY 29 | 62 |
| DAY 28 | 60 | DAY 30 | 64 |

AFFIRMATION GLOSSARY 67
COLORING BOOK PAGES 69
ABOUT THE AUTHOR... 133

Introduction

EVERY WOMAN IS A SPECIAL GIFT CREATED BY GOD, AND THE DIVINE essence within her should be self recognized. However, this has not always been an easy task for me and many other women. At age 63, I have experienced not recognizing my self worth and had times where I sought unnecessary validation from others. This was not good for me and essentially prevented me from embracing my full potential as a woman with dreams.

I've struggled immensely with maintaining high self esteem, not second guessing myself at every turn, being comfortable in who I am, and accepting love from those that genuinely had my best interest at heart. I stopped to ask myself, "why am I always doing this?" My answer was staring me in the face, but I just wasn't ready to face reality.

I was listening and giving all of my energy to prioritizing the opinions of family members who I loved. Eventually I realized that the issue was my lack of faith in myself. I needed to remind myself of the meaning of believing.

The word "belief" is a powerful word and should never be used lightly. Having belief in myself was the missing piece to my life as a woman. This was blocking me from expressing the talents I naturally possessed. Believing in myself was a struggle that continued to hold me back from seeing and accepting the power in me that was always there. This was the case until I received the opportunity to tell my story to the world. I began to get excited thinking about all of the beautiful older women that needed encouragement just like me. I learned to recognize the determination, drive, energy, and power I possessed and all the phenomenal ways that I could be a vessel to inspire other older women to love themselves more, treat themselves to the joys of life, recognize their worth, and be unapologetic in who they are.

Please know that you are not slowing down and preparing for the end; instead you are just getting started to walk the runway, showcasing how beautiful you are inside and out, and that you are ready to take the seat on the throne of your new life!

A Guide To Using My Journal

SELF LOVE IS IMPORTANT TO EVERY WOMAN AND MAINTAINING IT requires confidence, consistency, and determination.

Sometimes we as women begin to lose and give up on ourselves, easily inviting negative thoughts and talk into our hearts and minds.

Journaling is one of the best ways to start your day positively and get you excited about all the great things that will make your day incredible.

Using my journal and affirmations together will uplift you, make you smile, boost your confidence, make your day productive, and leave you feeling vibrant. You will realize the importance of never giving up on yourself while being reminded that you are the most important person in your life.

Daily Quick Steps to Getting Started

Each day that you begin to use the daily affirmations remember to follow through with the journal question for the day to maintain a positive and healthy life as a woman in her new phase of life. The purpose of the daily affirmations is to keep you on the right path even when you have negative thoughts that discourage you about the love you have for yourself. When you use the affirmations and journal together, you are communicating with your mind, body, and soul as a powerful and strong woman.

1. Before placing your feet on the floor in the morning, take about 5 minutes to speak aloud your affirmation energetically.
2. Read each affirmation daily, preferably in the morning. Maybe over a cup of coffee, tea, or juice.
3. Look in the mirror and say the affirmation.
4. Repeat the affirmation for extra assurance to show self love.
5. Look in the mirror and wrap your arms around your body as you repeat the affirmation.
6. Give yourself a warm smile after each affirmation and breathe deeply to show satisfaction.
7. Think of a special place that reminds you that you deserve all the love that is offered to you.

10 Suggested places to post your affirmation for the day as a reminder of self love.

1. Calendar
2. Bathroom Mirror
3. Coffee Pot
4. Cell Phone Case
5. Closet Door
6. Refrigerator
7. Microwave
8. Sun visor in the car
9. Steering wheel
10. Computer

DAY 1

"I choose to embrace all of me today."

1. "I choose to embrace all of me today." Recall 3 ways you embraced yourself today.

DAY 2

"I will not apologize for being me."

2. You are beautiful and not apologetic for this. List down reasons you are unapologetic about being you.

DAY 3

"I love and appreciate myself. I am who I am and I love me for it."

3. "I love and appreciate myself. I am who I am and I love me for it." How do you feel when loving yourself?

DAY 4

"I am an amazing gift to myself, my friends, and the world. I am too awesome to wallow in self-pity."

4. Write a letter to two friends that feel you are an amazing gift to them, thanking them for their presence in your life.

DAY 5

"Today I feel endless empathy
and love for all those in
my circle of positivity."

5. Being beautiful and compassionate demonstrates a confident woman. Think about a moment when you felt beautiful.

_____
_____
_____
_____
_____
_____
_____

Think about a moment you felt compassionate.

_____
_____
_____
_____
_____
_____
_____

DAY 6

"I hold the key to my life and the joy it brings."

6. Recall the most recent time love was given to you and how you knew you deserved it.

DAY 7

"I do not need the company of others
to feel complete.
I am more than enough.
I enjoy my solitude."

1. List 5 women in your circle of positivity that you have endless empathy and love for.

DAY 8

"I am a queen that radiates happiness when she enters the room."

8. Today you will show self love by repeating today's affirmation 3 times while you look in the mirror. Describe how you feel.

DAY 9

"I am allowed to feel good. I am on fire with self-confidence."

9. Feeling beautiful is a part of your inner confidence. What is something you will do today to show yourself how beautiful you are in your own skin?

DAY 10

"I begin this journey in my life to explore my voice. I allow myself the freedom to express the depths of my feelings."

10. A queen that radiates happiness when she enters a room is powerful. Describe a moment when you entered a room and all eyes were on you.

DAY 11

"I can achieve all things if I keep trying, even when it gets challenging."

11. "Today I am on fire with confidence because…"

DAY 12

"I will not give up until I have tried everything, and when I have tried everything, I will look for other ways to try."

12. Reflect on a time when you were trying to achieve something in your life but you became frustrated. Did you give up? Why or why not?

DAY 13

"I will not criticize myself. I will love myself for who I am and for what I have become."

13. Reflect on a time you criticized yourself. How did you feel?_____

DAY 14

"I am not only enough, I am *more* than enough. I also get better every day I live. Tomorrow I will be a better version of myself than I am today."

14. Describe what a better version of you looks like.

DAY 15

"I am growing at my own pace."

15. Recall when you discovered that you were growing at your own pace. Visually describe this feeling.

DAY 16

"The older I get, the more I will let go of my worries over things that I cannot control.
I will instead focus my energy on what I can control."

16. What are some things you can control in your life?

What are some things you cannot control in your life?

DAY 17

"I wake up every morning with hope for the day.
I start my day out embodying what I want to give and what I want to receive."

17. List one thing you want to give to others.
    List one thing you want to receive.

DAY 18

"My inner beauty is as talented, gifted, creative, and original as my outer beauty."

18. Compare and contrast your inner and outer beauty.

DAY 19

"Today is the beginning of whatever I want."

19. How do you want your day to begin for you? Describe.

DAY 20

"Only my thoughts are my reality.
I will focus on the good
and not the negative."

20. Think about YOUR most breathtaking dream that seemed so real. What details of that dream actually felt like your reality?

DAY 21

"I embrace change and rise to the new opportunities it presents."

21. Reflect on changes you have made in your life recently. List the most significant change that has impacted your life.

DAY 22

"I will relax my mind and stop thinking of false stories in my life. I will allow my mind to unwind while being at peace."

22. Think of a place where you would love to go to relax your mind without interruptions. Why is this destination the best place to relax and avoid interruptions?

DAY 23

"Today I celebrate my crown of life, peace within my soul."

23. Describe your Crown of life celebration.

DAY 24

"It is too early to give up on my dreams."

24. What would cause you to give up on your dreams?

DAY 25

"I am bold, beautiful, and sexy! Definitely the woman I need to be."

25. What kind of woman do you feel you need to be and why?

DAY 26

"My self-esteem encourages me to spread my wings and continue to succeed at being me."

26. Describe your self esteem.

DAY 27

"I am confident in the trust I have in myself to make wise decisions today."

21. What is the amount of trust you have in yourself?

DAY 28

"The higher I climb, the more positive I feel and the stronger my self-esteem grows."

28. Describe the positive feeling you get as your self-esteem grows.

DAY 29

"I am me, you are you. Trust in God, He'll see you through the journey you have planned for you. Take your time and leave the stress behind."

29. What plans do you have to reach your destination?

DAY 30

"Let your dreams be your source of energy."

30. Are your dreams your source of energy?

Affirmation Glossary

CROWN OF LIFE (PAGES 2 AND 5)

The Crown of Life is referred to in James 1:12 and Revelation 2:10; It is bestowed upon **"those who persevere under trials."** Jesus references this crown when he tells the Church in Smyrna to "not be afraid of what you are about to suffer... Be faithful even to the point of death, and I will give you the crown of life."

CIRCLE OF POSITIVITY (PAGES 1 AND 3)

Your circle is made up of the people you surround yourself with in your life and can include your family, your friends, work colleagues or people you associate with through personal activities or your business.

Coloring Book Pages

About The Author

Meet 13th and Joan author Deborah Ware. Born and raised in New Orleans, Louisiana, Deborah is a mother of three sons, a grandmother of 8, and wife to retired army Sergeant John Ware. Deborah is a fifth grade English Language Arts teacher in Gwinnett County who is a natural at creating stories and songs. This is demonstrated in her first book, "Breaking Chains." Aside from being a teacher and author, Deborah is a singer/songwriter, inspirational encourager, and believer that beauty is not only on the outside but also on the inside.

  Deborah loves to dream and use her dreams to inspire others who struggle with self-confidence. Her goal is to encourage older women to believe in themselves and to pursue their dreams, while recognizing the fact that, with age, life is not over; instead, it's more vibrant and just beginning!

To learn more about Deborah, follow her on all social media platforms at

@iamtherealdeborahware
and on her official website
www.iamtherealdeborahware.com

www.ingramcontent.com/pod-product-compliance
Lightning Source LLC
Chambersburg PA
CBHW071146060526
44107CB00132B/229